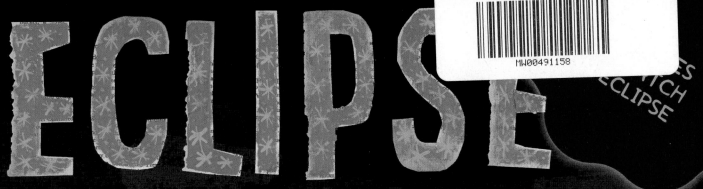

ECLIPSE

How the 1919 Solar Eclipse Proved Einstein's Theory of General Relativity

Moments in Science

Written by
Darcy Pattison
& Illustrated by
Peter Willis

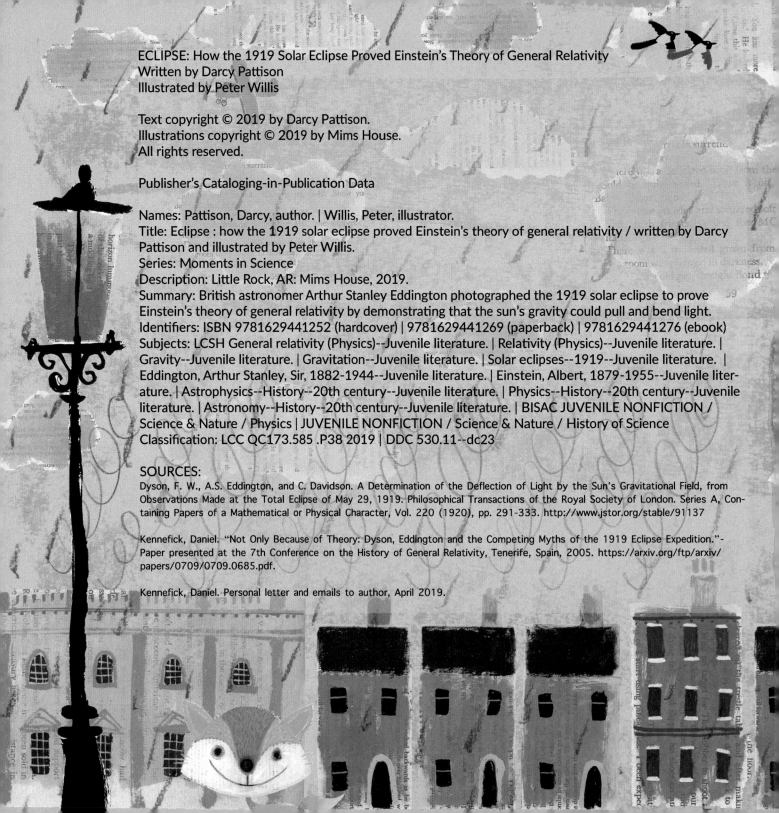

ECLIPSE: How the 1919 Solar Eclipse Proved Einstein's Theory of General Relativity
Written by Darcy Pattison
Illustrated by Peter Willis

Publisher's Cataloging-in-Publication Data

Names: Pattison, Darcy, author. | Willis, Peter, illustrator.
Title: Eclipse : how the 1919 solar eclipse proved Einstein's theory of general relativity / written by Darcy Pattison and illustrated by Peter Willis.
Series: Moments in Science
Description: Little Rock, AR: Mims House, 2019.
Summary: British astronomer Arthur Stanley Eddington photographed the 1919 solar eclipse to prove Einstein's theory of general relativity by demonstrating that the sun's gravity could pull and bend light.
Identifiers: ISBN 9781629441252 (hardcover) | 9781629441269 (paperback) | 9781629441276 (ebook)
Subjects: LCSH General relativity (Physics)--Juvenile literature. | Relativity (Physics)--Juvenile literature. | Gravity--Juvenile literature. | Gravitation--Juvenile literature. | Solar eclipses--1919--Juvenile literature. | Eddington, Arthur Stanley, Sir, 1882-1944--Juvenile literature. | Einstein, Albert, 1879-1955--Juvenile literature. | Astrophysics--History--20th century--Juvenile literature. | Physics--History--20th century--Juvenile literature. | Astronomy--History--20th century--Juvenile literature. | BISAC JUVENILE NONFICTION / Science & Nature / Physics | JUVENILE NONFICTION / Science & Nature / History of Science
Classification: LCC QC173.585 .P38 2019 | DDC 530.11--dc23

SOURCES:
Dyson, F. W., A.S. Eddington, and C. Davidson. A Determination of the Deflection of Light by the Sun's Gravitational Field, from Observations Made at the Total Eclipse of May 29, 1919. Philosophical Transactions of the Royal Society of London. Series A, Containing Papers of a Mathematical or Physical Character, Vol. 220 (1920), pp. 291-333. http://www.jstor.org/stable/91137

Kennefick, Daniel. "Not Only Because of Theory: Dyson, Eddington and the Competing Myths of the 1919 Eclipse Expedition."- Paper presented at the 7th Conference on the History of General Relativity, Tenerife, Spain, 2005. https://arxiv.org/ftp/arxiv/papers/0709/0709.0685.pdf.

Kennefick, Daniel. Personal letter and emails to author, April 2019.

A SOLAR ECLIPSE IS WHEN THE MOON MOVES BETWEEN THE EARTH AND THE SUN.

It's a scientific fact. During a rainstorm, you can't see the sun, the moon, or the stars. Or a solar eclipse.

WHAT IS AN ECLIPSE?

During an eclipse, the moon's shadow makes part of the earth dark. As the moon travels across the sun's path, the sun looks like a shrinking crescent. Finally, the sun is totally black with only a corona, or glowing light, around the edge. When the sun is totally blocked by the moon, it's called the totality. Totality only lasts a couple of minutes. As the moon keeps moving, the sun is a growing crescent until the moon has completely passed. To see an eclipse, you must travel to the places where the moon's shadow falls. And hope the skies are clear.

British astronomer, or star scientist, Stanley Eddington needed to see the May 29, 1919 solar eclipse. He planned to photograph distant stars during the eclipse and change science forever.

SIR ARTHUR STANLEY EDDINGTON (1882–1944), known as Stanley, was a British astrophysicist, a scientist who studies the stars and physics. A Quaker, he was a conscientious objector to World War I. He was excused from military service because of his astronomy work. Stanley was the head of the Cambridge Observatory. He joined Frank Dyson, the director of the Greenwich Observatory, to plan an expedition to Príncipe Island to photograph the 1919 solar eclipse. Stanley was also known for his work on what makes up the insides of stars, the luminosity of stars, and other theories.

His plans to photograph the 1919 solar eclipse started four years earlier. German scientist Albert Einstein was studying how forces

PUSH
and
PULL

objects in space. On November 25, 1915, Einstein explained to other scientists his new theory of general relativity.

WHAT IS A THEORY?
A theory is an explanation of something in science. When a theory is first developed, it might later be proved to be a scientific fact, or not. A theory needs observations, experiments, and other evidence to prove it. Developing and testing theories is what science is all about.

Apparent location of star

Path of starlight

Real location of star

Earth

Gravity is a force that  **PULLS** an object toward another object.

At the time, scientists thought that light traveled in a straight line. But Einstein said something startling. He said that the sun's huge gravity pulled and bent light. To prove his new theory, he needed observations from an astronomer like Stanley Eddington.

EXAMPLE OF GRAVITY
Earth has a strong gravity. If you throw a ball up, earth's gravity pulls the ball back down to the ground.

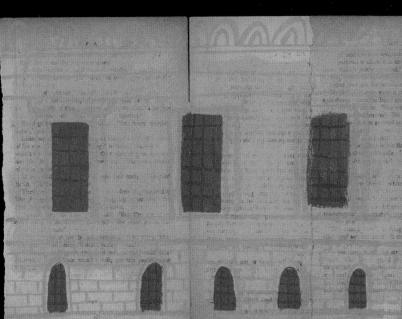

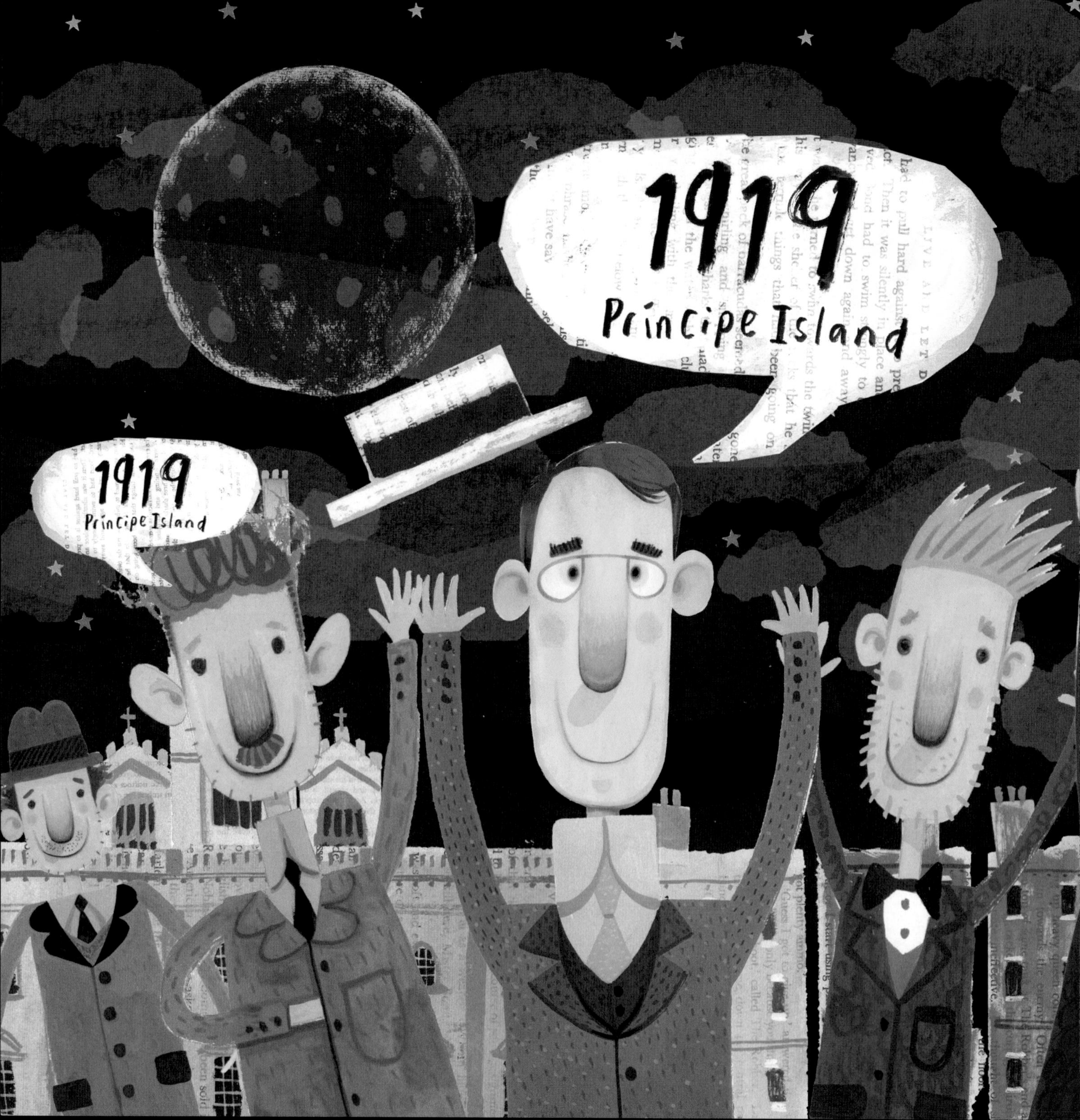

Stanley and other astronomers decided to try to measure light bending around the sun's gravity by photographing a solar eclipse.

1919
Príncipe Island

HOW TO MEASURE LIGHT BENDING

If Einstein's theory was right, light was bending around the sun all the time. But to measure light bending, scientists needed a solar eclipse to block out the bright sun so they could photograph stars in the background. They would need two sets of photographs of stars. First, the astronomers took photos of the stars before the eclipse. These are the NON-ECLIPSE photos. Then, they took DURING-ECLIPSE photos. Finally, they would compare the NON-ECLIPSE and DURING-ECLIPSE photos. If the stars' position appeared to move, it meant the starlight had bent.

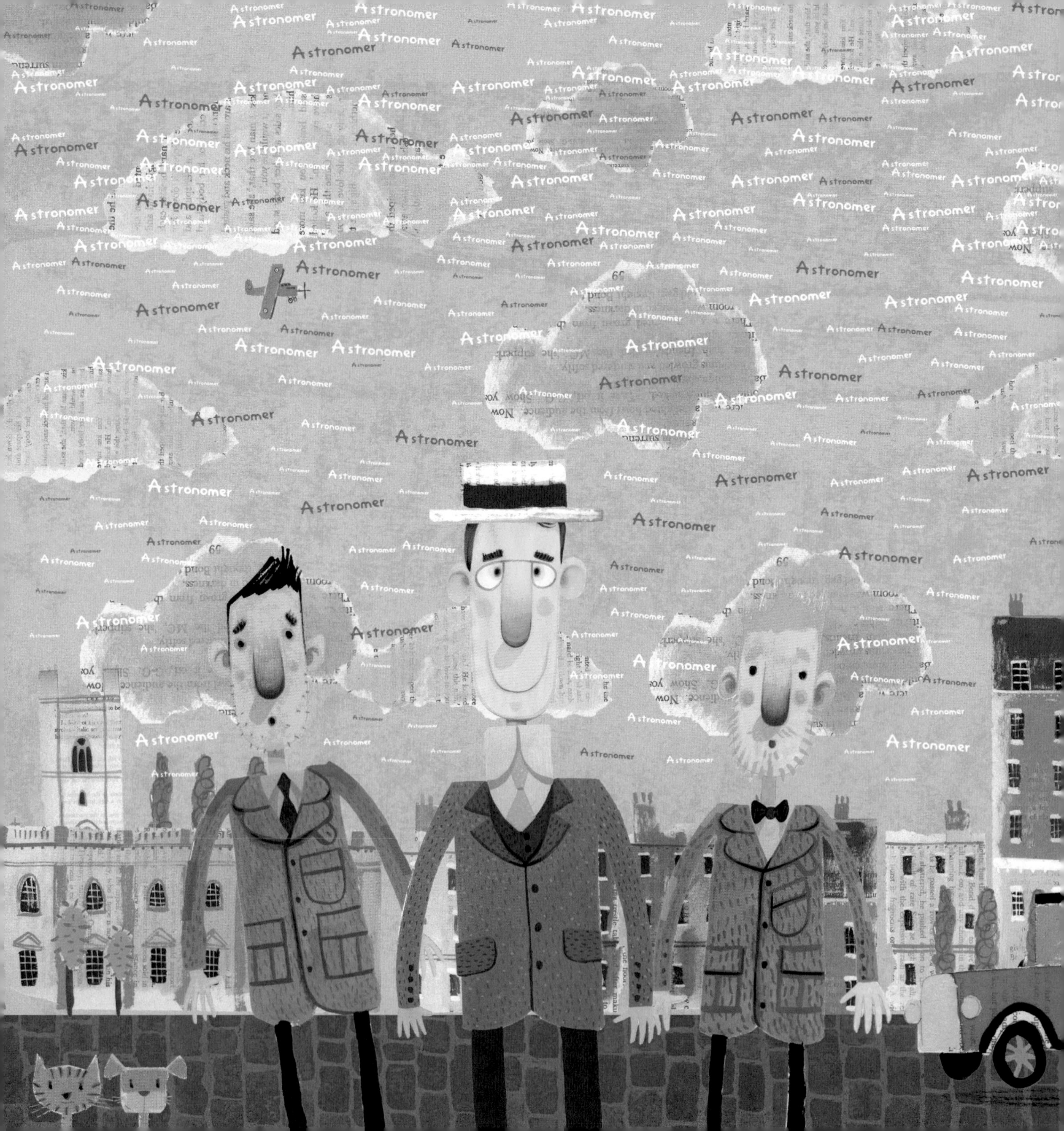
Astronomer

THE 1919
ECLIPSE
WOULD BE A
PERFECT
TIME TO MEASURE
LIGHT BENDING.

WHY THE 1919 ECLIPSE?

The 1919 eclipse was a perfect time to measure light bending because of two scientific facts. First, the totality—the time the sun would be totally blocked by the moon at Príncipe Island—would be very long: 5 minutes and 2 seconds, or about the time it takes to say, "astronomer" 302 times. They would have time to take many photographs. Second, the stars behind the sun would be the bright Hyades star cluster. Bright stars would show up better in the photographs.

Hyades star Cluster

Aldebaran—
Taurus the Bull
constellations's
fiery eye

Before leaving England, the scientists photographed the Hyades star cluster for the **NON-ECLIPSE** photos.

Starting in March 1919, Stanley took a 47-day boat trip from England to the tiny island of Príncipe, just off the coast of Africa. On Príncipe, he would have the best view of the eclipse. Traveling with Stanley was Edwin Cottingham, a clockworks expert.

Edwin was in charge of the complicated moving parts of the telescope. They also sent an expedition to Brazil to photograph the eclipse from there.

PHOTOGRAPHING STARS IN 1919

was hard. A 10-by-8-inch (25.4 x 20.32 cm) piece of glass, called a glass plate, was coated with special chemicals. The glass plate was inserted into a slot in the telescope behind a piece of cardboard that blocked light. To take a photo, Stanley pulled out the cardboard for a certain amount of time to let the light hit the glass plate. To stop the exposure, he replaced the cardboard. To take the next photo, he had to change the glass plate. Stanley had a schedule for taking photos and planned to alternate 5-second and 10-second exposures. Later, Stanley would dip the glass plates into special chemicals to develop the photograph, or to make it show up.

On the morning of May 29, clouds massed in the gloomy sky, and a tremendous rain storm came on. Would it clear in time for the afternoon eclipse?

About noon, the rain stopped. The sky started to slowly clear. Stanley and Edwin hopefully set up the telescope.

They waited until about 1:30 p.m. when the clouds finally cleared. The eclipse had already started! The sun was a glimmering crescent.

As the sky darkened from the moon's passage, the stars came out.

When totality, or total darkness, started, they called out, "Go!"

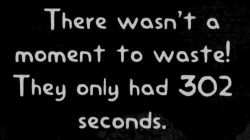

There wasn't a moment to waste! They only had 302 seconds.

They started a metronome, a simple machine that clicks off the seconds. Tick. Tick. Tick. Tick. Edwin watched the telescope to make sure all the equipment worked correctly.

ECLIPSE SAFETY:
You should never look directly at the sun, because it can blind you. Even during an eclipse, when the sun is almost completely hidden, it is dangerous to look at.

Stanley pulled out the
cardboard and exposed
the photographic glass
plate for **5** seconds.
Tick, tick, tick, tick, tick.

Tick, Tick,
Tick, Tick
Tick, Tick,
Tick, Tick

Quickly, he switched to a new plate. He exposed the new plate for 10 seconds.

Tick, tick, tick, tick, tick, tick, tick, tick, tick, tick.

Time rushed by. Stanley worked for the full 302 seconds, taking 16 photos.

Later, Stanley developed the photos on the glass plates. On the last 6 photos, stars glittered behind the eclipse. He packed the photos carefully for the trip back to England. There, he spent hours measuring the Brazil and Príncipe photos, comparing and calculating.

THE BRAZIL TEAM

A second team of astronomers was sent to Sobral, Brazil to photograph the solar eclipse. Surely, they hoped, at least one location would have clear skies. Charles Davidson, an expert on telescopes, led the Brazil expedition. With him was Irish astronomer Andrew Crommelin, an expert on comets. The Brazil expedition had a full-size telescope similar to the Príncipe expedition. But the telescope warped in the heat, and the photos were fuzzy. Their backup telescope was smaller, with only a 4-inch (10.16 cm) lens. The small telescope produced the best photographs of either expedition and were important in measuring the light bending.

Finally, on November 6, 1919, Stanley and other astronomers announced the results of their eclipse observations. Light bent around the sun! The photos said that Einstein's general theory of relativity was correct.

Science has never been the same. For years after and still today, scientists would argue about Einstein's theory. But Stanley knew one thing: starlight bends around the sun.

He had measured it.
It's a scientific fact.

Original photograph from the May 29, 1919 total solar eclipse.
This shows the position of the stars as dim horizontal lines.
Image is in the public domain.

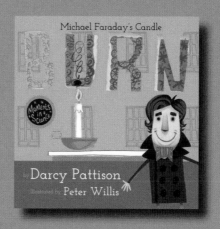

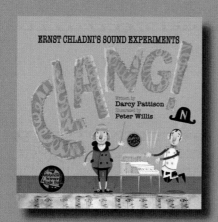

READ THE AWARD-WINNING SERIES

MOMENTS IN SCIENCE

Clang! 2019 NSTA Outstanding Science Trade Book

Pollen Starred Kirkus Review and
Junior Library Guild Selection

Made in the USA
Monee, IL
01 April 2024

56185793R00021